HOW BREAD IS MADE

I WONDER
HOW BREAD IS MADE

Neil Curtis and Peter Greenland

Lerner Publications Company • Minneapolis

This edition published 1992
by Lerner Publications Company
241 First Avenue North
Minneapolis, Minnesota 55401 USA

Original edition published in 1990 by Heinemann Educational
Books Ltd., Halley Court, Jordan Hill, Oxford OX28EJ England
Copyright © 1990 by Heinemann Educational Books Ltd.

Library of Congress Cataloging-in-Publication Data

Curtis, Neil.
    How bread is made / Neil Curtis and Peter Greenland.
        p.   cm.—(I wonder)
    Originally published: Oxford, England : Heinemann
Educational Books, 1990.
    Summary: Describes how bread is made, illustrating the
process that begins in a wheat field and ends at a bakery.
    ISBN 0-8225-2375-2
    1. Bread—Juvenile literature. 2. Wheat—Juvenile literature.
3. Bakers and bakeries—Juvenile literature. [1. Bread. 2. Wheat.
3. Bakers and bakeries.] I. Greenland, Peter. II. Title. III. Series:
Curtis, Neil. I wonder.
TX769.C84 1992
641.8′15—dc20   91-24388
                                                        CIP
                                                        AC

Manufactured in the United States of America.

1 2 3 4 5 6 7 8 9 10 01 00 99 98 97 96 95 94 93 92

Bread is the most common food in the world.
It is made from many different ingredients
and comes in many different shapes.

Most of the bread we buy in stores
is made from wheat.
Wheat is a kind of grass.

Farmers grow wheat in large fields.
First the farmer needs to loosen the dirt.
A tractor pulls a plow that turns the dirt over.

Then the dirt must be leveled
and the big lumps broken down.

This time the tractor pulls a harrow behind it.
The harrow's sharp blades break down the lumps.

Next the farmer plants the wheat seeds.
A seed drill digs rows in the soil
and drops seeds into the rows.

When the wheat starts to grow,
the bright green sprouts
look like blades of grass.

With plenty of rain and sunshine,
the wheat will grow quickly.
It will grow to be almost five feet (1½ meters) tall.

After seeds develop, the wheat dries out
and turns a golden-brown color.
It is ready to be harvested, or cut.

The farmer harvests the wheat
with a machine called a combine.
The combine cuts the wheat
and separates the seeds from the stems.

Dry stems of wheat are called straw.
Straw is rolled into bales.
Farmers use the straw to make warm beds for
cows, horses, and other farm animals.

The combine blows the wheat seeds,
or kernels, into a truck.
Then the kernels are taken to a flour mill.

At the mill, the kernels are ground into
flour and put into bags.

Then bakeries buy the flour to make bread dough.

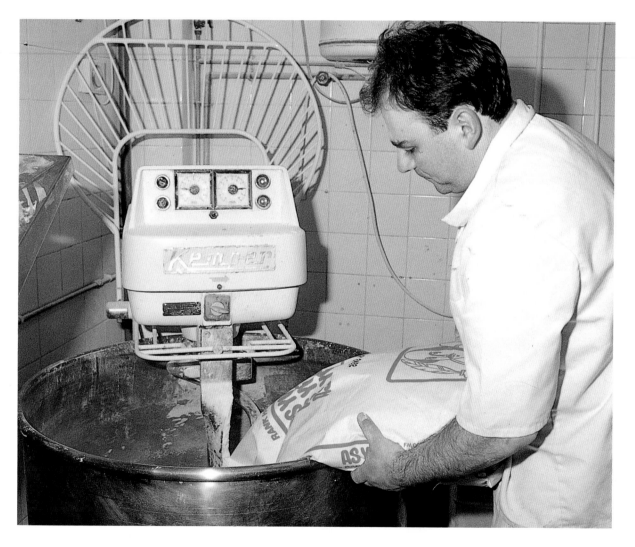

Dough is made by mixing flour, water, and salt.

The baker adds yeast to the dough.
Yeast is a kind of living plant.
The yeast will grow and
make the dough rise.

First the dough is mixed by special machines.
Then the dough is put in a warm place
and allowed to rise.
Warm air helps the yeast grow faster.

After the dough has risen,
the baker cuts it into pieces.
The pieces are put into baking pans.

The baker shapes some of the dough by hand.
There are lots of ways to shape dough.

The dough is allowed to rise again.

When the dough is puffy,
the baker puts it into big, hot ovens.
The dough bakes into bread.

The baker takes the warm, crusty bread
out of the oven.
The bread will be sold from the bakery,
or it will go to other stores that sell fresh bread.